Hitler's Daughter

THE PLAY

Adapted by Eva Di Cesare,
Sandra Eldridge and Tim McGarry

FROM THE NOVEL BY JACKIE FRENCH

Currency Press,
Sydney

CURRENCY TEENAGE SERIES

First published in 2007
by Currency Press Pty Ltd,
Gadigal Land, Suite 310, 46–56 Kippax Street, Surry Hills, NSW 2010, Australia
enquiries@currency.com.au
www.currency.com.au

Reprinted 2009, 2011, 2013, 2015, 2017, 2022, 2024.

Cataloguing-in-Publication data for this title is available from the National Library of Australia website: www.nla.gov.au

Currency Press acknowledges the Traditional Owners of the Country on which we live and work. We pay our respects to all Aboriginal and Torres Strait Islander Elders, past and present.

Eva Di Cesare, **Sandra Eldridge** and **Tim McGarry** were three actors sitting in a Darlinghurst coffee shop on a wet and windy April morning in 1997. It seems an unlikely place for the birth of a theatre company, but that's exactly where the seeds of Monkey Baa were first sown. During its first tour of *The Bugalugs Bum Thief* (adapted from the book by Tim Winton) in 1998 in a long wheelbase van, the cast lugged a heavy set into classrooms, libraries and community halls across Australia, performing to over 15,000 young people. And with that Monkey Baa Theatre Company was born. Since then, they have been creating inspiring, award-winning theatre for young audiences. They have adapted over 15 classic Australian stories for the stage, with the common thread through all work that young people's interests are valued and respected. They strive to ensure that young people, wherever they are located and whatever their economic circumstances, have the opportunity to share in fantastic theatre experiences that reflect their own lives. Now one of Australia's largest touring companies, Monkey Baa has conducted over 25 national tours to 135 regional and remote communities across every state and territory of Australia, 3 international tours and over 2,500 performances, and engaged with 1.2 million young people. As resident company at the Lendlease Darling Quarter Theatre, they curate an annual season of theatre for young people, presenting Monkey Baa plays and work from other Australian and international companies.

Jackie French's writing career spans eighteen years, 48 wombats, 130 books, translations into twenty three languages, over 50 awards in Australia and overseas, and 27 chewed up back doormats. (Wombats love chewing doormats.) She is one of the few writers to win both literary and children's choice awards. *Hitler's Daughter* won the Australian 2000 CBC Book of the Year for Younger Readers, the UK Wow! Award, a Semi Grand Prize Award in Japan and has been listed as a 'blue ribbon' book in the USA. It has featured in the shortlists for the various children's choice awards around Australia every year since it was first released.

Read more about Jackie at www.jackiefrench.com, or sign up for her free monthly newsletter at www.harpercollins.com. au/jackiefrench.

Mikaela Martin (left) as Fraulein Gelber and Tahli Corin as Heidi in the 2006 Monkey Baa production. (Photo: Heidrun Löhr)

Contents

Typeset for Currency Press by Dean Nottle.
Printed by CanPrint Communications, Canberra ACT.
Cover design by Kate Florance, Currency Press.
Front cover: Tahli Corin as Heidi. Back cover: Nathan Carter as Frau Leib, Tahli Corin as Heidi and Matt Goodwin as Mark. Both photographs from the 2006 Monkey Baa production. Photographs: Heidrun Löhr.

Publication of this title was assisted by the Commonwealth Government through the Australia Council, its arts funding and advisory body.

Foreword

When Eva, Sandie and Tim from Monkey Baa approached me to put *Hitler's Daughter* on the stage, I didn't think it could be done. How can you put modern kids in a flooded country valley as well as war-ravaged Berlin on stage? It's easy in a novel ... tell people it's the Berlin of 1945, or that the floodwaters are brown and frothy, and there you are. How can you put a man with a small moustache and long leather boots on stage and call him Hitler without someone giggling?

And then I saw a dress rehearsal. I heard the rain and saw the bombs, felt the shadow of Hitler not just looming over the theatre but wherever people still want to blindly follow leaders who offer them hope or excitement.

It was exactly the world I had written about, and suddenly I was there and so was everyone else in the theatre. Even knowing exactly how they did it still doesn't quite explain the magic of the production.

The play isn't the book, just as the book isn't the play. Each will give you something different. But the heart of both are the same. And there is no way I can thank the team at Monkey Baa for the extraordinary gift of seeing the world in my mind's eye upon the stage, for producing a play that left audiences silent in shock and wonder for twenty seconds before they began to applaud. They were brilliant. Simply and utterly brilliant.

Jackie French

First Production

Hitler's Daughter was first produced by Monkey Baa Theatre for Young People at The George Fairfax Studio, The Arts Centre, Melbourne, on 26 April 2006, with the following cast:

Mark / Soldier	Matt Goodwin
Anna / Mum / Fraulein Gelber	Mikaela Martin
Tracey / Heidi	Tahli Corin
Ben / Dad / Frau Mundt / Mr McDonald / Frau Leib / Mrs Latter / Driver	Nathan Carter
Recorded Voice-over of Hitler	Markus Weber

Director, Sandra Eldridge
Designer, Imogen Ross
Lighting Designer, Luiz Pampolha
Sound Designer, Jeremy Silver
Stage Manager, Zillah Morrow
Dialect Coach, Jennifer West

German translation for the original production by Markus Weber.

German translation for the published manuscript by Wolf von Kehler.

Acknowledgements

The adaptors wish to acknowledge Jackie French for her wonderful story, all her support, and for being such an inspiring person.

Many thanks to Noel Jordan from the Sydney Opera House for introducing us to Jackie French's *Hitler's Daughter*.

Monkey Baa also wishes to thank the Sydney Opera House Youth and Education Program for their assistance in the creative development of the production.

And a very special thank you to Avril Alba and Olga Horak at the Sydney Jewish Museum.

A Note from the Adaptors

One of our chief aims when establishing Monkey Baa ten years ago was to encourage the appreciation of Australian literature in young people. We do this by taking novels from highly respected authors, such as Tim Winton, Morris Gleitzman, Gillian Rubinstein and Andrew Daddo, and adapting them for the stage, thereby giving the audience the opportunity to view a story in two different forms: on the page and on the stage. Jackie French's novel *Hitler's Daughter* is our fifth such adaptation, but our first foray into creating a play for a teenage demographic.

We had been in discussion with Noel Jordan, Head of Young Audiences at the Sydney Opera House, and he presented us with several novels that he felt might work as stage adaptations. One of these novels was Jackie French's *Hitler's Daughter*. We were captivated by it on first reading, and we all felt compelled to adapt it. Often, in searching for a piece to adapt, the three of us read up to sixty or seventy books, spending months tossing around possibilities, and eventually rejecting novels because we can't find a common thread. With *Hitler's Daughter*, we couldn't wait to start!

With all three of us having a keen interest in history, we were excited by the novel's blend of fact and fiction. Very much an Australian story, we were drawn to the novel's juxtaposition of a kind of contemporary ordinariness with an extraordinary time in world history. We loved the story's provocative questions about the manipulation of society in the 1930s and 1940s, and the way the story forced us to question our identity and the world we inhabit. As human beings, how can we overcome the wrongs of the past and forge new paths? Can we honestly and openly face the wrongs, recognise the wrong paths taken in the past and thereby avoid taking the wrong turn again?

We were captivated by the way the chief protagonist, Mark, becomes absorbed by the events in Nazi Germany, and his reflections on contemporary issues: How do we know our parents are doing the right thing? Was our land acquired at the expense of indigenous Australians? We wanted to create a script that moved the audience to explore the play's themes and ask themselves the same questions that Mark asked himself. Each character in the story offered a different moral perspective, but we didn't want the play to provide concrete, or easy, answers.

We were also excited by the practical challenge of creating two worlds simultaneously on stage: Germany in the 1940s and the Australian bush in the present day. As a small theatre company, we were restricted by a multitude of factors. We needed to create a touring production on an incredibly limited budget that could bump into a theatre in less than four hours, and with only four actors playing all fourteen characters. We were blessed with a highly talented creative team who took on this challenge with fervor and brought our adaptation to life.

We began the adaptation in late 2004. Throughout the process the script was sent back and forth to author Jackie French for suggestions and feedback. During the Sydney Writers' Festival in May 2005, the company conducted a series of creative development workshops as part of the Sydney Opera House Youth and Education Program. High school students shared their thoughts and feelings about the play's themes of racism, prejudice, genocide, generational guilt and responsibility.

And then in 2006, *Hitler's Daughter* toured to 33 theatres throughout five states across Australia, playing to an audience of 24,000 young people. In tandem with the touring production and in collaboration with The Sydney Jewish Museum, the company toured an exhibition of images of the holocaust and testimonials from survivors.

In adapting the novel we not only wanted to capture its 'feel', but stay true to the author's vision, original plot and character journeys, ensuring that the play would enhance the visual images conjured when reading the novel. We feel proud of the final script and are deeply indebted to Jackie French for entrusting us with her stunning story.

Eva Di Cesare, Sandra Eldridge and Tim McGarry

A Note from the Director

We had fourteen characters, four actors to play them, two worlds to create – Germany in the 1940s and a bus stop in the Australian bush – plus it was to be a touring show that had to bump into theatres in less than four hours and we had to depict one of the most evil men to ever live. Now... where to begin? Our first achievement was assembling the dedicated, passionate and talented creative team of Imogen Ross, Luiz Pampolha and Jeremy Silver.

As adaptors we had made certain staging decisions whilst creating the script of *Hitler's Daughter*. We wanted the staging to be relatively simple, and we tried to ensure that objects on stage were multifunctional. The bus stop bench, for example, became, in turn, Mark's mother's car, a German SS car, the school bus, and the single bed in the final bunker scene. Decisions reached during the writing process 'fed' the early design meetings. With the creative team, it was decided that the bus stop would also become Hitler's bunker and this effect was beautifully created by simply dropping a solitary light bulb into the bunker scene.

During my own 'dreamtime' I kept imagining a tree on the stage. In our research we discovered that there was actually a tree planted in the driveway of Berchtesgaden, Hitler's country residence (and a later setting in the stage play), specifically planted to shade Hitler during the parades that marched past him. This was just one of many coincidences that happened throughout the design process that reinforced the design and staging decisions. So we had a tree. I also explored children's stories, specifically German fairytales, and what began to appear again and again were the woods and forests where shadows of monsters dwell and, metaphorically speaking, where we all have to venture in our journey for the truth. The stage design began to develop, and with more trees we now had both the German woods and the Australian bush, where our bus shelter sat innocently like a gingerbread house with its yellow tin roof.

Like a book itself, we envisaged each side of the shelter opening out to reveal other places and times in the story, with Mark's farmhouse and Heidi's home mirroring each other and representing, in part, how the past is always there in the present and the possibility of inhabiting the consciousness of another time through objects.

The challenge of how to depict Hitler was solved during the adaptation process. Hitler was sometimes portrayed in the 1940s as the evil shadow over Europe and it seemed accurate to represent him as that, a huge shadow lit up on the back cyclorama. In keeping with my fairytale readings, Hitler became the big black monster of many guises, evil in its many forms, the darkness that dwells in human kind. The hanging of a cyclorama at the back of the stage meant that we could incorporate other lighting effects to reinforce the factual nature of the story – a swastika, the symbol of Nazism, and a map of Germany in the 1940s clearly displaying the concentration camps where horrific crimes against humanity took place. At times we flooded the stage with the colours of the German flag when we were in Germany and the red of the swastika also echoing blood on the land, whilst in Australia we chose more cool blues to reflect a world cold and wet, and one not often associated with Australia. We also were interested in the colours of the past, going against the sepia tones of memory, often evoked by photographs. The past then did not become a separate place.

The fall of Berlin was created with strobe flashes. These flashes lit up the trees and brought them alive so that shadows thrown onto the cyclorama became the soldiers and the buildings falling. Accompanying the lighting, sound effects were constructed from everyday sounds, roadwork drills and the like, thus blurring the past and present. Sounds of the woods and shadows of leaves upon the stage also added to the depiction of our two worlds.

The staging challenges were great with only four actors covering multiple roles. I came to rehearsal with some specific ideas regarding the transitions. I was interested in exploring the notions of times crossing and characters weaving in and out of the stories and the worlds. This raised the possibility of both Mark and Heidi meeting briefly, the past and present worlds gently colliding.

It was set up very early in the piece that the actors, by physical and vocal transformation, could become other characters in front of the audience. Anna could enter the story that she was telling and become the character of Fraulein Gelber. Tracey could change her posture, remove a coat and become Heidi. It became an acceptable theatrical device in the storytelling and very exciting for the actors, and hopefully, the audience too.

We rehearsed *Hitler's Daughter* in four weeks. The actors, Matt Goodwin, Nathan Carter, Mikaela Martin and Tahli Corin, were all extraordinary, bringing to rehearsal great ideas and most importantly enthusiasm. I am entirely grateful and thankful to them for their trust and creativity in bringing this story alive.

Directing *Hitler's Daughter* was a great honour. In the times that we live it takes courage and even humour to consciously look for the good in life. To place ourselves on the side of the caring, the kind, and have empathy and compassion for others is important. By acknowledging our responsibility for humanity, we can embrace the past and enhance our future, not just as individuals but as a race, the human race.

Sandra Eldridge
Director
Monkey Baa Theatre production, 2006

Characters

In Australia:

Mark, 11 years old, quiet and intelligent. A bit of a loner.
Ben, 11 years old, boisterous, loud, rude and funny.
Anna, 11 years old, quiet, serious, highly intelligent and thoughtful. Compelled to tell her story.
Tracey, 8 years old, enthusiastic and bubbly, with a happy-go-lucky disposition.
Mum, 30s, a farmer's wife. Works locally at the grain store in town.
Mr McDonald, 30s, a teacher at Mark's school.
Dad, 30s, an Australian farmer, stoic and kind.
Mrs Latter, 50s, school bus driver. Loud, opinionated lefty who wears woolly beanies.

In Germany:

Heidi, ages from 9 to 11 years old through the play. She is Hitler's daughter. Small and dark like her father, she has a birthmark on her face and a pronounced limp. She speaks with a soft German accent.
Fraulein Gelber, 30s, a thin German woman, carer and tutor to Heidi. She speaks with a soft German accent. Contained and strict yet kind. She has dedicated her life to the Führer.
Frau Mundt, 40–60 years old. Head cook and housekeeper at Berchtesgaden. She dresses in traditional German dress. She speaks with a hard German accent.
Driver, a member of the SS.
Frau Leib, 70s, peasant farmer's wife. A gossip, married to a man who was one of the early members of the Nazi Party.
Soldier

Hitler was depicted in the original production as a shadow, and his lines were delivered as a voice-over.

Prologue

We hear HEIDI singing a gentle verse of 'Twinkle Twinkle Little Star' in German:

Heidi *Funkel, funkel, kleiner Stern,*
Ach wie bist du mir so fern,
Wunderschön und unbekannt,
Wie ein strahlend' Diamant,
Funkel, funkel, kleiner Stern,
Ach wie bist du mir so fern.

The lights come up to reveal HEIDI sitting on the ground in front of one of the trees.

As the song finishes, the light fades and we hear heavy rain.

Scene 1

Early Tuesday morning.

The lights come up on a bus shelter somewhere in the Australian countryside.

The sound of heavy rain on the yellow tin roof of the bus shelter.

The crack of thunder and lightning. A car door slams. The car drives off.

MARK, wet, appears and runs to the bus shelter. He stands alone.

We hear a cow mooing nearby.

BEN bolts into the bus shelter, soaked. His frenetic energy is the antithesis of MARK's stillness.

Ben Hey, move your bag!

He throws his bag which hits the back wall of the shelter with a thud.

Check out the creek. It's all gone yellow. The bridge'll go if this keeps up.

A flash of lightning.

Mark Hey, Ben, have you ever noticed that cows look all shiny when they're wet?

Ben Nuh.

He sneezes.

Mark Like someone's polished them. Do you think cows can sneeze?

Ben Nuh.

Mark How come they can't, then?

Ben Dunno.

Mark Maybe they only sneeze when we're not around.

Ben Whatever?

BEN scrapes the mud off his boots.

Mark It's just they're kind of sad looking—wet cows.

Ben Hey, there's Anna. Her mum must have picked up Tracey too.

Two car doors slam shut offstage. The car skids off.

ANNA and TRACEY run into the bus shelter. ANNA carries both backpacks and holds TRACEY's hand.

Anna Hi, Mark.

Mark Hey, Anna, have you ever heard a cow sneeze?

Anna No.

Mark Maybe if a cow had hay fever, it'd sneeze.

Tracey Come on, Anna...

Anna Later, Tracey.

Mark What?

Tracey If the bus is late, Anna says we can play the game again.

Ben Which game?

Anna The one I used to play with my grandma.

Tracey You know, we make up a character and Anna makes up the story.

Ben Boring.

Mark There's nothing else to do.

Tracey I want a story about a fairy... or a pony.

Ben How about something good like some dude that steals a million bucks and—?

Mark How about a dinosaur? A Pteranadon?

Tracey Yeah. A baby one. A baby Pteranadon called Billie. She gets separated from her mother and—

Ben Blerck!

Anna I'll choose this time.

Mark You? But you never choose.

Anna Then it's my turn, isn't it?

Ben Just make it something good. No fairies or fish or crap like the last time.

Mark The bus'll be here if you don't shut up. Go on, what's the story going to be about?

Anna It's about... it's about Hitler's daughter.

Ben Hey, cool.

Tracey Who's Hitler?

Ben Hitler? He was this bloke in World War Two. He was the leader of Germany and they were the enemy. He had all these Brown Shirts and the Gestapo and they tortured people and had concentration camps and everyone had to go 'Seig Heil' or 'Heil Hitler'! You know, like in those movies on TV.

Mark But Hitler didn't have a daughter.

Ben So what? Hitler's heaps better than a stupid old Pteranadon. Who cares if he had a kid or not?

Mark But... but we can't have a story about something that's not real.

Ben Why not? Fairies and other crap like that aren't real, are they?

Tracey They are too real.

Mark No, of course not. But... it's just different when you make stuff up about a real person. It's just... Okay then, what was Hitler's daughter's name?

Ben Buffy.

Mark You so got that from TV.

Ben So what?

Mark You can't have someone from TV in the game. Anyway, Buffy isn't German.

Anna Austrian. Hitler was Austrian.

Ben What's the difference? Who knows any Austrian names?

Tracey Her name was Heidi.

Ben Tracey, that's from that boring book.

Mark Give it a rest, Ben. Let's just get on with the story. The bus'll be here soon. Okay, Anna. Her name was Heidi and she was Hitler's daughter.

Tracey And she lived in a castle.

BEN groans.

Anna Not really. But it was big with wide terraces and so many rooms that... that Heidi could never count them. And then there were the 'don't go down there' rooms where Duffi talked with people in uniforms and flowery dresses.

Ben Who was Duffi?

Anna Hitler.

Ben Duffi?

Anna I don't know why she called him Duffi. I don't even know if it means anything. It was just what she did.

Ben Yawn. Get to the good bit.

Anna Duffi's own rooms were upstairs but she wasn't allowed to go there either. When Duffi visited he came to her rooms instead.

Tracey What were Heidi's rooms like?

Ben Who cares? Get to the battles. You know, the Russian front or Rommel in Egypt.

Anna I don't know about any battles or the Russian front. He kept her away from all of that. Look, this isn't going to work. Hitler's daughter was a stupid idea. Forget I started it. Okay. How about another story? Tracey, you can choose.

Tracey But I want the story about Heidi.

Anna Okay. Let's make her a princess. Princess Heidi...

Tracey No, I want a story about the other Heidi. The one you were talking about.

Anna But... Oh, all right then. But I can't tell you anything about battles. She never saw any battles.

Ben She must have! She was Hitler's daughter.

Anna He kept her away from the battles. He kept her away from everyone. No one knew about Heidi. She lived with Fraulein Gelber at Berchtesgaden—that was where Hitler had a house in the country and that was the only world she knew.

Mark But why?

Ben Oh, man, what does it matter? It's only a story.

Mark Why did he keep her a secret?

Anna Because she had a birthmark... across her face. And she had a limp. She wasn't perfect and Hitler wanted to breed the perfect race... tall children with blue eyes and blond hair who could run and jump and conquer the world. His daughter was small and dark like him.

Tracey Then he didn't love her.

Mark Of course not. He was Hitler. I bet Hitler never loved anyone.

Anna I don't know if he loved her or not. She always hoped he did.

Mark But someone like Hitler couldn't... How many people did he kill?

A bus screeches to a halt.

Ben Bus. That story's weird.

Anna I said it wasn't working.

Tracey It's not weird. I like it.

BEN exits and TRACEY follows him.

Mark Anna?

Anna Yeah, what?

Mark What happen to Heidi's mum?

Anna I think she died. She must've died. Heidi never knew her.

Mark Will you go on with the story tomorrow?

Anna Yes... no... maybe. If it's raining.

Mark Why don't we get down here earlier tomorrow so you've got more time?

Anna I thought you didn't like it.

Mark It's all right.

The sound of a bus horn.

They exit to the bus.

Scene 2

The driveway of Mark's farm. Early Wednesday morning.

The sound of heavy rain.

MARK runs to the car with a coat over his head and a piece of toast, the remnants of his breakfast.

Mark Come on, Mum. I'll be late for the bus.

MUM runs to the car with an umbrella.

Mum We've got ages yet.

Mark But it'll be slower because it's muddy. Anyway, I need to talk to Anna about a project for school.

Mum That water tank will overflow if this goes on.

They both get into the Volkswagen.

We hear MUM turn on the ignition. The radio comes on. MUM backs the car out of the driveway.

Radio 'The Prime Minister today announced that he was committed to maintaining troop levels overseas despite protest from the Opposition. The further deployment of up to one thousand members of the elite wing of the land forces is now being discussed in relation to the recent revelations that...'

Mum Mark, radio off, please. Not listening to the news this morning. Too depressing. Got your homework?

Mark Yep. Mum?

Mum Mmm?

The car hits a pothole and bounces. MUM grunts.

Mark What's the longest time it's ever rained?

Mum I don't know... Noah's flood. Forty days and forty nights. Oh, and for six weeks back in forty-seven, so your nanna told me. Fog and rain for six weeks.

Mark Six sevens are forty-two... that beats Noah's by two days. [*Beat.*] Did it flood?

Mum Right up to the garden fence where the vegie garden is now. Nanna said no one could get out for weeks.

The car hits another big puddle.

Oops, sorry about that. Oh, look at that cow... Get off the road, you stupid creature.

Mark Hey, Mum. Do cows ever sneeze?

Mum Mmm... What was that? I don't think so.

Mark Why not?

Mum No idea.

Mark Mum? What do you know about Hitler?

The car hits another puddle.

Mum Bugger... Hitler? What brought that up?

Mark What was he like?

Mum Oh, Mark, not now... It's bad enough trying to keep the car on the road.

Mark Please, Mum.

Mum He was a monster. All the concentration camps... He killed all those Jews... six million, I think.

Mark Six million people?

Mum It's called the Holocaust. He killed lots of others, too... even disabled people. There was a TV program on it last year, but we turned over to a movie halfway through... Something like eleven million people all up.

Mark Eleven million? That's more than half the population of Australia.

Mum They weren't just in Germany... there were also camps in all the other countries he invaded. It was a long time ago, Mark.

The sound of the rain stops.

The car bounces through another puddle.

Bugger! That nearly hit the sump.

Mark But why?

Mum What do you mean why?

Mark Why did he do it?

Mum That was the sort of person he was.

Mark But he must have had a reason!

Mum I think he wanted to breed a super race. He called it the Aryan Race. So he had to get rid of anyone who was different... Oh, look out, you silly roo—

Mark How could someone like that run a country?

Mum I don't know.

Pause.

Mark Can I jump out here? It's stopped raining.
Mum There's still a way to go.
Mark I don't mind. I'll walk.
Mum All right, then.

MUM stops the car.

Mark See ya.
Mum See you tonight. Are you sure you got your homework?
Mark Yep, I'm sure.
Mum And your lunch money? Mark?

MUM indicates for MARK to kiss her on the cheek. He does so reluctantly.

MARK walks towards the bus stop deep in thought.

The lights fade on MUM as the Volkswagen is heard driving off.

Scene 3

The bus shelter. Early Wednesday morning.

MARK arrives. TRACEY and ANNA are already there.

Mark Morning.
Tracey Hi, Mark.
Mark Your story's been bugging me all night.
Anna Really?
Mark Yeah... and it's like you don't want to tell it at all.
Tracey Yes she does. Don't you, Anna? I got my mum to drop us off extra early.
Mark It's like Heidi seems real.
Anna It's just a story.
Tracey Go on, Anna, go on with the story. You said you would. Didn't you, Anna?
Anna All right!
Mark Yeah. Better get a move on before Ben gets here.

Anna I don't think Ben's coming today. He's got a cold. His mum rang my mum so I could tell the bus driver not to wait for him.

Tracey Go on, then!

Anna I'm not sure where to start.

Mark What did she do?

Anna I don't know.

Tracey Well, did she have any pets... a dog? A pony?

Anna No.

Tracey Did she go to school?

Anna No, no she didn't go to school.

Mark Why not?

Anna Because... because people might discover Hitler had a daughter. Or they might tease her about the mark on her face.

Tracey Did she go anywhere?

Anna She went to church, I think. I don't know. This is just not working.

Mark How about start with, 'As far back as she could remember...'

Tracey As far back as Heidi could remember...

Anna As far back as Heidi could remember there was Duffi.

Tracey Duffi.

Anna Duffi was the Führer, and he was her father too. No one said he was her father. She never called him 'vater'. She called him Duffi and he hugged her whenever he visited, which wasn't often, and he brought her dolls with long blonde hair that made her secretly cry at night.

Mark Why?

Anna Because they were beautiful and she was not.

Mark But how did she know she was Hitler's daughter if he never said?

Anna I don't know. She just did. She lived there in his house—or the house he visited sometimes when he wasn't in Berlin—and he called her 'my little girl'. 'How is my little girl today? Has she been good for Fraulein Gelber?'

Heidi Oh, yes, Duffi.

Anna In the mornings she did her lessons with Fraulein Gelber.

Mark Who was Fraulein Gelber?

Anna Fraulein Gelber looked after her. She was tall and thin, with hips that looked like she had a coathanger in her skirt, and she had dark hair pulled back and wore narrow skirts that meant she couldn't walk or run too fast. After her lessons Heidi would go walking with Fraulein Gelber in the afternoons.

Germany. Summer, 1944. Berchtesgaden. In the gardens.

The lights change.

A cuckoo call.

Fraulein Gelber That's a cuckoo's call! Listen, there's a thrush.
Heidi Fraulein Gelber… the pond, the pond.

HEIDI rushes to the pond.

Fraulein Gelber Heidi, you walk too quickly.

FRAULEIN GELBER follows her. HEIDI throws bread into the pond.

That carp is so big.
Heidi They don't seem to like the bread today.
Fraulein Gelber Perhaps they are not so hungry.

FRAULEIN GELBER prepares to read Mein Kampf.

Heidi Fraulein, I would really like to go to school, with other girls.
Fraulein Gelber Oh, dear child, you know that is not permitted.
Heidi But I never see anyone.
Fraulein Gelber But you are such a lucky girl, you know that. All these wonderful things you are learning. You have such pretty things too, and a lovely home, good food, and you have Duffi who loves you just as he loves all his German children. Now, the daily read from the Führer's own hand.
Both *Mein Kampf.*
Heidi I hope that one day he will tell me that he loves me the best.
Fraulein Gelber I am sure he will, my child, I am sure he will.

She exits.

The bus shelter.

The lights change.

Above: From left, Matt Goodwin as Mark, Mikaela Martin as Anna and Tahli Corin as Tracey. Below: From left, Matt Goodwin as Mark, Mikaela Martin as Fraulein Gelber and Tahli Corin as Heidi. From the 2006 Monkey Baa production. (Photos: Heidrun Löhr)

Mark What…? How could she want someone like that to love her?

Anna He was her father.

Mark But he did so many terrible things. What about the concentration camps? What about all the Jews he killed and the war and how he invaded Poland and all that?

Anna She didn't know.

Mark But she must have!

Anna The concentration camps were secret. What they did there was a secret. They were just supposed to be work camps. That's what it said in the newspapers and no one showed them to her except when her father made a speech. Fraulein Gelber would cut out his photo for her to pin on the wall. How would she know what was happening? She didn't even go to school so she couldn't listen to other people talk.

Mark But she was there—in Hitler's house—in the middle of everything.

Anna She was in the middle of everything but she knew less than anyone outside. She knew there was war. People talked about the war. But no one said it was Hitler's fault. Frau Mundt, an old widow who worked in Hitler's household, thought he was wonderful.

Germany, 1944. Berchtesgaden. The kitchen.

The lights change.

FRAU MUNDT enters, mixing a cake in a bowl. She talks to HEIDI.

Throughout the following speech we can hear the cheering masses at a Nazi rally.

A swastika fades up on the backdrop with the sound of the crowd.

Frau Mundt Before the Führer we had no work, no bread. Even money was worth nothing in those days. A wheelbarrow full of money wouldn't buy you a loaf of bread. We begged. It was horrible… we had to beg just to get food to eat. The occupying troops, the French and the Belgians, took all we had. Then it was 1932. I went to hear the Führer give a great speech. He wasn't the

Führer then but it was so wonderful—thousands of people… oh, so many people cheering.

He told us how he wanted to be on the side of the unemployed. He would save us, he would get us jobs, he would make Germany proud and free again, and I was cheering with everyone while the tears ran down my cheeks.

That night I prayed that this great, good man would get all the votes so he could get us out of need. No one else promised what he did. No one. He was the only one who gave us hope. This good man. And everything he has promised, he has given us.

She gives HEIDI the spoon to lick as they exit.

The bus shelter.

The lights change.

Anna Hitler was the leader who was going to save Germany, who would bring about the Third Reich. Germany would reign over the world and all the shame of World War One would be wiped out.

Mark But the shame was wiped out before World War Two. Germany had the Olympics.

Anna Hitler wouldn't shake that guy's hand… Jesse Owens.

Mark Because he was black.

Anna Yes. There was one time when Heidi realised something was wrong. One of the women in the kitchen was wailing, 'I didn't know. I didn't know. They took her away. They said it was for the best, she would be cared for.'

Germany. 1944. Berchtesgaden. The hallway.

The lights change.

A map of Europe fades up on the cyclorama clearly depicting the concentration camps.

Heidi Frau Mundt. What's wrong with Freya?

Frau Mundt She has just found out that her sister is dead.

Heidi When did she die? In the air raids?

Frau Mundt Her sister was not quite right. In the head, you understand, not clever like other children. So they took her to a special place. No one told the family she had died, not until they wrote to say they would visit next month. And now Freya thinks they have killed her sister there.

Heidi Did they kill her?

Frau Mundt No, of course not. Of course they didn't. Freya has just been listening to stories—silly stories, you know how people talk. But sometimes, sometimes things like that have to happen. It's for the good of everyone. We cannot have weaklings in the new German race. People like Freya's sister mustn't be allowed to have children. It's like it is with the Jews.

Heidi What are Jews?

Frau Mundt The Jews are different. They are different from us. That is why the Führer wants to separate them. So they cannot endanger the life blood of the German people, so they cannot weaken it.

Heidi What happens to them?

Frau Mundt They are sent to camps. Places to work.

Heidi Are there any Jews near here?

Frau Mundt No, of course not. But if one did escape and come near here the guards would catch them and send them back. There is no need to worry.

Heidi I'm not worried.

The bus shelter.

The lights change.

Anna And why would she worry? Why would Heidi believe any differently?

Mark If she'd just started to think about it all—

Anna Would you know if your parents were doing something wrong?

Mark Of course I would. But they wouldn't do anything really wrong.

Anna Are you sure? All the things your mum and dad believe in—have you ever really wondered if they're right or wrong? Or do you think they're right because that's what they say, so… so it has to be right?

Mark Well, I… [*Pause.*] It's not the same.

MARK exits in anger. ANNA exits following him.

Anna Mark!

Scene 4

The playground. Wednesday afternoon.

The lights change.

We hear the school siren. It echoes a World War Two air-raid siren.

MR MCDONALD is rushing across the playground with a briefcase in his hand.

Mark Mr McDonald?

Mr McDonald Make it quick, Mark.

Mark I just wanted to know… I mean, it's dumb, but I was thinking, do kids have to be like their parents?

Mr McDonald I'm not sure I get your meaning.

Mark Well, say someone's father did something really evil. Would their kids be evil too?

Mr McDonald No, they probably wouldn't be evil too.

Mark But, we're like our parents, aren't we?

Mr McDonald Yes and no, you inherit your talents from your parents, but what you do with them is your choice.

Mark So… so Hitler's kids, for example. They wouldn't go round killing people?

Mr McDonald There isn't any trouble at home, is there, Mark?

Mark No! I mean no, I was just wondering. I saw something on TV about Hitler, that's all, and I wondered if he had a son, what he'd be like.

Mr McDonald Hitler didn't have any kids.

Mark But if he did? It wouldn't be his fault, would it? All the murders his dad did?

Mr McDonald No, it wouldn't be his fault at all. Not unless he felt the same way as his dad did. Or maybe if he refused to face up to the evil things his dad had done… that would be wrong. If we don't face up to things that were wrong in the past then we might do them again. Okay, Mark?

MR MCDONALD goes to exit.

Mark Mr McDonald…

Mr McDonald Yes, Mark?

Mark The things Hitler did… all that genocide stuff. I mean, could he have ever thought he was right?

Mr McDonald I don't know. Sometimes people think they are doing the right thing even when it is bad. But with Hitler I just don't know.

Mark But how can we *know* we're doing the right thing?

Mr McDonald I can't answer that either. I had better go, I've got an after-school staff meeting. No more questions, then?

He exits.

Mark No more questions.

Scene 5

A farmhouse kitchen. Dusk. Wednesday.

A screen door slams.

The lights change.

Mum Is that you, Mark?

Mark Yeah, home, Mum.

Mum Gee, that bus was late today.

Mark No, no I just walked slow.

Mum You all right, mate?

Mark What? Oh, yeah, I'm okay.

DAD enters repairing an old radio. MUM exits.

Dad?

Dad Mmm? Mark, if it's trigonometry, ask your mum. You know what I'm like at maths.

Mark No, it's not homework. I was just wondering…

Dad Just let me finish this bit, will you?... Wondering what?

Mark Why did Hitler hate the Jews so much.

Dad What's brought this on?

He stops repairing the radio.

Mark Oh, just something at school.

Dad No idea. He killed anyone who disagreed with him, too.

He resumes repairing the radio.

Mark Dad?

Dad Yep?

Mark If you were Hitler...

Dad If I was *who*?

Mark No, Dad, I'm serious. If you did things like Hitler did—really bad things—what do you think I should do?

Dad You mean should you go along with me 'cause I'm your dad, no matter what?

Nathan Carter (left) as Dad and Matt Goodwin as Mark in the 2006 Monkey Baa production. (Photo: Heidrun Löhr)

Mark Yeah, that's about it.

Dad I don't know. I s'pose I'd want you to do what you thought was right. But... if we do disagree, I hope we'll still be able to sit down and talk about it, no matter how much we row. That it, mate?

Mark I don't know. Hey, what would you do if I was a mass murderer? You know, chopped up people with a chainsaw or something.

Dad Stop your pocket money. And I'll tell you straight, kid, you murder one more person and there'll be no more TV for a fortnight. And you'd better clean the blood off my good chainsaw, too.

Mark No, really.

Dad Dunno. Try and work out why you did it. Be sad for you. Be sad for your victims. Try and get you help. Wonder how your mother and I failed you.

Mark Would you turn me in to the police?

Dad Yes. I s'pose I'd have to. That's a hell of a question, mate.

Mark Would you still love me?

Dad Mark.

Mark No matter what I did? Even if I killed hundreds and hundreds of people?

Dad Of course we would, you goose... or maybe we'd love you in a different way... What's brought all this on, anyway?

Mark Oh, nothing.

DAD exits.

MARK begins to play with the radio, searching for a station.

Suddenly from the radio comes the sound of thousands of people chanting 'Sieg Heil'.

He stares at the radio in horror.

A strobe lighting sequence accompanies the chanting.

MARK, frightened, exits.

The chant on the radio bleeds into the sound of heavy rain as the lights crossfade into the next scene.

Scene 6

The bus shelter. Early Thursday morning.

Continual heavy rain can be heard.

Tracey Where's Ben?

Mark Still sick, I guess. This is never gonna stop. It's gonna go on and on and all the cars will float away and we'll have to catch a boat to school.

Tracey Really?

Mark Of course not really. Hey, Anna... I was wondering... have you told anyone else this story? The Hitler one?

Anna No. It's just between us.

Tracey Yeah... our little secret.

Pause.

Mark Are you going to tell us more?

Pause.

Anna It was soon after Heidi asked about the Jews, that they had to move house.

Germany. Autumn, 1944. Berchtesgaden. Heidi's bedroom.

The lights change.

Heidi Why do we have to go?

FRAULEIN GELBER waves a letter at HEIDI too quickly for HEIDI to read it.

Is it from Duffi?

FRAULEIN GELBER shrugs her head and hides the letter in her pocket.

Where are we going to?

Fraulein Gelber We will look it up on the map in the car. It will be a nice place. You will like it.

Heidi A car! But why do we have to go?

Fraulein Gelber It will be safer there… and it's much nearer my family.

Heidi Will they visit us?

Fraulein Gelber I don't think they'll visit.

Heidi Will Duffi visit? Will he be at the new house?

Fraulein Gelber No, of course not. He is in Berlin. Driver?

Heidi But he will visit?

Fraulein Gelber *Vielleicht*, perhaps. [*Calling offstage*] Driver, the cases!

The DRIVER enters carrying suitcases.

They get into the car.

Fraulein Gelber How long is the drive?

Driver One hour.

They drive.

Heidi Look, Fraulein, goats. [*To the DRIVER*] Can we stop?

Fraulein Gelber Shush. You mustn't talk to the driver.

Silence.

The humming of an aeroplane.

The humming gets louder.

The DRIVER pulls the car off into the gravel.

Perhaps we should just get out and lie on the ground. What if they see the car?

Driver Too late.

Heidi Will we hear the sound of the bomb falling before it kills us?

Terrified, HEIDI cranes to look. FRAULEIN GELBER pulls her back. They hold each other. The DRIVER braces for the bomb to fall.

As the plane approaches louder, its black shadow crosses them from above. The plane's engine fades to a hum.

They relax from their brace positions. The DRIVER starts the car and their journey continues.

Why does that house have cardboard for windows?

Driver Stray bomb. Sometimes they have a few spare they haven't dropped on targets so they drop them anywhere. They don't use up so much fuel carrying them home.

Heidi Where is home?

Driver England. England is the enemy.

Heidi Are they evil people or just stupid? How can they possibly win against all of Germany, against Duffi?

The bus shelter.

The lights change. The two scenes run concurrently.

Mark So the Germans thought the English were evil?

Heidi Will we make it to our new home?

Mark But didn't they know?

Heidi England is the enemy.

The DRIVER parks the car. He exits with the cases.

Mark But Hitler was the evil one.

Germany. Autumn, 1944. A farmhouse in the woods.

The lights change.

Fraulein Gelber This new house is small. But it has three bedrooms upstairs. One for me, one for you, Heidi, and the third will be our schoolroom.

Mark But the Germans bombed England, didn't they?

Fraulein Gelber There is a cellar you can go to out the kitchen door and down some steps. Bombs may crush the house, but the cellar will be safe.

Heidi Look at all these jars of plum jam and sauerkraut and honey. So much food. Where are the people who lived here before?

Fraulein Gelber That's none of our business.

Heidi It seems odd to be eating their food, not knowing where they are.

Fraulein Gelber *Genug!* [Enough!] A woman will come tomorrow to cook and look after the house. Her name is Frau Leib. She is just a farm woman, but I want you to be polite to her, even so.

Above: From left, Tahli Corin as Heidi, Mikaela Martin as Fraulein Gelber and Nathan Carter as the Driver. Below: From left, Matt Goodwin as Mark, Mikaela Martin as Fraulein Gelber and Tahli Corin as Heidi. From the 2006 Monkey Baa production. (Photos: Heidrun Löhr)

Heidi Yes, Fraulein Gelber.

Fraulein Gelber Frau Leib has been told that you are my niece, the child of my sister who was killed in the air raids.

Heidi Was your sister killed in the air raids?

Fraulein Gelber Of course not, my sister is quite well. Apart from a slight case of grippe last month. But it's best if that's what Frau Leib continues to believe. I don't want you speaking too much to her, you understand?

Scene 7

The bus shelter.

The sound of rain pounding the bus shelter roof. A cow moans softly.

Mark Go on.

Anna The bus...

Mark We've got another five minutes at least. Go on!

ANNA takes a deep breath and begins the story again.

The lights change.

FRAU LEIB enters, gathering firewood.

Anna Frau Leib had grey hair, not speckled like Fraulein Gelber's but grey all over like a saucepan, and tight curls that looked like they were made of metal too, they were so firm on her head. Her hands were large, with red knuckles.

Mark And did she live with Heidi and Fraulein Gelber?

Anna No, Frau Leib lived on a farm just down the road, the one with the pigs in the black mud. Her husband, Herr Leib, was in the Nazi Party—one of the first members in the district—so his wife was supposed to be trustworthy. But Frau Leib... she loved to gossip.

Germany. Autumn, 1944. The woods.

The lights change.

Frau Leib What happened to your face, girl? A burn? Is that what it is? The bombs?

Heidi I was born with it.

Frau Leib You poor darling. I will give you some ointment. It's pig lard, with chickweed and other herbs. It is my grandmother's recipe and she got it from her mother, so it is very good. It takes scars like that away so fast you'd think the boar was after them to get back its fat.

Heidi *Dankeschön.*

Frau Leib Shh. Listen to the frog in the pond. If frogs croak like that at night it will rain in the morning.

Heidi Are there fish in the pond?

Frau Leib Just the frogs. [*She drops the firewood.*] Oh, we need help. All the fine, strong men are in the army, and just the old men and boys to help us now. If the farm had been bigger my sons might have stayed so they could help the Führer by growing food for all the soldiers of the Reich. Of course, they are proud to be fighting too. We all have to do what we can.

A plane is heard flying low over the woods. It flies over them.

HEIDI jumps up to wave. FRAU LEIB pulls her down.

Heidi I could almost see his face.

FRAU LEIB spits on the ground.

Frau Leib I have brought you a present.

Heidi What is it?

Frau Leib Here in my pocket.

HEIDI looks deep into FRAU LEIB's apron pocket.

Heidi A rabbit!

Frau Leib It's a doe. When she gets bigger you can breed it with a buck and then you'll have lots of rabbits and I'll show you how to make rabbit pie.

Heidi *Dankeschön.*

Frau Leib You're a good girl.

She exits.

The bus shelter.

The lights change.

Tracey Rabbit pie? You can't eat a rabbit.

Anna It was the war. People were trading saucepans for an egg or even jewellery for a hen. Everything was rationed.

Mark Wasn't Hitler a vegetarian?

Tracey Poor rabbit.

Scene 8

The school bus. Thursday morning.

The sound of a bus horn. We hear the bus arrive.

Tracey Hi, Mrs Latter.

Mrs Latter Where's Ben?

Anna Still sick.

Mrs Latter Still?

The sound of the bus driving off.

I'd like to see the blinking Mayor drive this blinking road twice a day. [*She blows her nose.*] Made sure he got the bitumen right up to his place, no worries about that. But as for doing anything for us out here...

Mark Anna?

Anna Yeah, what?

Mark You know how Hitler went on about the Jews? Was there anything in it?

Anna Of course not!

Mark No, I don't mean about the Jews. But what I mean is, are some people better than others?

Anna You mean, is any group of people or race or a religion, better than other people?

Mark Yeah, like Ben's dad says that Asians are all criminals.

Mrs Latter Ben's father is a racist little rooster with maggots for brains and I'll tell you why.

The bus swerves around a pothole and they all grab the edges of their seats.

You just have to look at the statistics, but does anyone bother to do that? No, they just listen to what some twerp has said on TV and take it as gospel. Never mind if it's true or not. People just don't think that's the trouble. They don't look at the evidence. Never mind if anyone with half a brain in their heads— Get on the right side of the road, you flaming numbskull!

MRS LATTER sounds her horn.

Anna What do the statistics say, Mrs Latter?

Mrs Latter Asians have a lower crime rate than the rest of the population, that's what they say, and if you don't believe me you can look it up yourself. You look at the ten most wanted criminals in Australia! Not a dark skin among them. All white and all dumb...

Mark Mrs Latter, do you think there's any group of people who are better or worse than other people?

Mrs Latter Sure.

Mark Really. Who?

Mrs Latter Men. They're the worst group of people out there.

Mark But men aren't a group or a race or—

Mrs Latter What are they, then? Most crime is committed by men. Most car accidents are caused by men.

She counts on her fingers. The bus swerves.

Anna [*under her breath to MARK*] Now look what you've done.

Mrs Latter Men start the most wars, and fight in them too. Most of the people in prisons are men. You just have to look at the statistics! You know what I think? I think men should pay higher taxes to pay for all the damage they do. Women are naturally gentler, more co-operative— Move your rear, you great mug!

The bus brakes suddenly. They all scream.

All Mrs Latter!

Blackout.

Scene 9

Mark's kitchen. Friday morning.

Throughout this scene a storm is heard building outside.

Radio '... the genocide still continues. Eye witnesses now say that the death toll may number several thousands, with the numbers still rising as government troops...'

MARK turns the radio volume up.

Mum [*offstage*] Mark.

MARK turns the radio volume down but still listens intently.

Radio '... And to national interests. The Senate has rejected a further push for amendments to the Native Title Act which would remove the rights of Aboriginal people to negotiate agreements on land subject to native title claim. Despite the encroachment of colonisation and various industries, Aboriginal people have maintained their relationship to their land and their traditional laws...'

DAD enters tying his tie, dressing for a business meeting, and turns the radio off.

Mark Dad.

Dad Mmm?

Mark Are people being exterminated today?

Dad What?

Mark Being exterminated. You know, like Hitler and the Jews.

Dad No.

Mark But on the news it just said about people being killed...

Dad Can't say I've being following it.

Mark Dad?

Dad Now what?

Mark How did great great grandpa get our farm?

Dad What? He bought it.

Mark He didn't steal it from the Aborigines?

Dad Don't be ridiculous. Anyway, it wasn't like that in those days.

MUM enters with Mark's lunch-order bag and a pen.

Mum Vegemite or peanut butter?

Mark But what if he *did* take it from the Aboriginal people?

Mum Mark!

Mark But just suppose. It wouldn't be our fault, would it?

Dad Who's been feeding you all that stuff?

Mark I was just listening to the news, and someone said—

Dad The things they teach kids nowadays. Do-gooders poking their noses in.

Mark But, Dad—

Mum Mark, give it a rest, would you? Vegemite or peanut butter?

Mark Peanut butter.

Mum You sure you don't want a pie?

Mark No. No pie.

A clap of thunder is heard.

[*To DAD*] You told me that if we disagreed about anything we should talk about it. You said—

Dad Mate, I haven't got time for this.

DAD exits.

Mum Mark, that's enough.

Mark But, Mum, what if *everyone* thought a really bad person was right?! Like all the German people thought Hitler was right?

Mum I don't think all the German people thought Hitler was right.

Mark Did people protest?

Mum No idea. I suppose so... Here's your lunch order.

Mark Would you have protested?

Mum Of course.

Mark Even if it meant going to prison?

Mum What? No, I suppose so. Mark, for the love of mud... no more questions. It's too early.

Mark I'll walk to the bus stop.

Mum I'll drive you a bit later.

Mark No!

Pause. MARK exits.

Mum Mark, there's a storm brewing... Oh, that boy!

More thunder is heard.

Scene 10

The bush of Australia and the woods of Germany.

The worlds collide.

The following action takes place simultaneously. MARK is walking angrily through the Australian bush. HEIDI is walking through the German woods.

They see each other... and stop.

Mark [*to HEIDI*] Why didn't the Germans do anything? They can't have agreed with Hitler. Or not with everything he did. But they went along with it, 'til it was too late. They simply shut their eyes and let things happen.

He exits running into the bus shelter.

Scene 11

Germany, winter 1945. The woods.

The lights change.

The map of the concentration camps reappears on the cyclorama during this scene.

Frau Leib [*entering*] They sent him away! Just last night.

Heidi Sent who away?

Frau Leib Herr Henssel! He has a farm over past the mill. No one would have guessed! None of us guessed!

Heidi Guessed what?

Frau Leib His sister married a draper in the town. A *Jewish* draper. *Ja*. The sister and her husband disappeared a long time ago, and everyone thought, oh, they have been taken to the camps. Herr Henssel never spoke of them. But Herr Henssel has been sheltering his sister and her husband all the time! He has been hiding them so they wouldn't take them to the work camps! Someone must have seen, someone must have noticed, and they must have notified the authorities, because today they took him away—took them *all* away. Oh, it is awful.

Heidi If the Jews just go to the camps to work, why did Herr Henssel have to hide them? Are the camps so terrible?

FRAU LEIB shrugs.

Are there any Jews near here?

Frau Leib Not in our village, not anymore. But before the war, in town, there were the Solomons, of course, in the draper's shop—not that I ever went there, you understand. My husband would have been angry if I went to a Jewish shop. And there was Herr... oh, what was his name? The teacher at the school, and the doctor, not the new one, the old one. One of his children went to school with Gerta, who married my... But you know that, I showed you the photo of the wedding, and the Führer sent a copy of his book with his signature just inside the cover. I have sometimes taken it and looked inside. I have looked at it often. Such a wise, clever book. Not that I have ever read it. But now, of course, all the Jews have been sent to the camps... It's just awful.

FRAU LEIB exits.

Scene 12

The bus shelter. Friday morning.

Mark I've guessed what happens now.

Anna What?

Mark I bet Heidi organised some escape plan for the Jews from the concentration camp. Or she spies on Hitler and passes on the information.

Anna Would you spy on your father?

Mark No, but my dad isn't Hitler.

Anna How could she spy on him? It had been months since she'd seen him. And even then, for just a few minutes. Who would she pass information on to? Besides, she didn't even know they were all meant to be killed in the camps.

Pause.

Mark But, she did try to help them?

Anna Sort of. She made a plan. She'd keep a watch out for any Jews who came to their garden, who needed help. And she'd hide them. It was easy at first. She told Fraulein Gelber...

Heidi I'm just going to clean out the hen-house.

Anna She shovelled out the muck. It was the first time she had held a spade and her hands became sore. She put down fresh straw. There had to be food, too. That was the next part of the plan. When they came to the garden for shelter she would have to feed them. She took jars from the cellar, just one each day. It took her a month, and then it was finished. Then she settled down to wait.

Mark When did the Jews come?

Pause.

Anna They never came. They were in concentration camps and very few escaped. But it was all she could do.

Mark But surely she could have done *something* else?

Anna What? Locked herself in her room and said she wasn't coming out or wouldn't eat 'til they shut down all the concentration camps?

Mark Yeah. Something like that.

Anna What good would have that have done? Do you think they would have paid any attention?

Mark But she was Hitler's daughter!

Anna But no one knew that and, besides, who listens to a kid?

Mark How will it finish? Will it go on and on 'til Heidi is grown up? Or does she die in the war?

Tracey No!

Mark But Hitler killed himself, and that woman he married right at the end of the war... Eva Braun... they both killed themselves.

Tracey No, that can't happen to Heidi. It can't!

Mark Anna can make the story turn out anyway she wants.

Germany. Winter, 1945. The farmhouse in the woods.

The lights change.

Fraulein Gelber We are going to meet the Führer. Quickly! Here's your coat. Your hair. Hurry!

Heidi It has been one whole year since I have seen Duffi!

Fraulein Gelber You are so lucky. With all his other concerns, the Führer still makes time to visit you!

The sound of motorbikes and cars on a gravel road. A car door slams and we hear footsteps on the gravel.

The headlights of the car create the shadow of HITLER.

HITLER's dialogue is heard as a voice-over in German.

Hitler [*voice-over*] *Nun Heidi, bist du ein braves Mädchen?* [Well, Heidi, have you been a good girl?]

Mark What is he saying?

Heidi Oh yes, Duffi. I have been a very good girl.

Hitler [*voice-over*] *Ist Fräulein Gelber gut zu dir?* [Fraulein Gelber has been good to you?]

Heidi She has been very good to me.

Hitler [*voice-over*] *Man kann ihr vertrauen. Es gibt wenige Menschen die vertrauenswürdig sind. Alle verraten mich! Alle!* [She can be trusted. So few people can be trusted. They are all betraying me. Do you know that, Heidi? All of them! All of them!]

Heidi I would never betray you. You can always trust me, Duffi.

Hitler [*voice-over*] *Sag mir Bescheid, wenn du irgend etwas brauchst.* [You let me know if there is anything you need.]

Heidi I don't need anything.

Hitler [*voice-over*] *Und höre auf Fräulein Gelber. Man kann ihr vertrauen, aber du musst immer wachsam sein.* [And you listen to Fraulein Gelber. She can be trusted. But you must always be on your guard.]

Heidi Yes, Duffi.

Hitler [*voice-over*] *Ich muss jetzt gehen, es gibt noch viel zu tun.* [I have to go. There is much to do.]

The sound of footsteps on gravel. A car door slams. The car drives off.

HEIDI salutes her father.

Heidi Goodbye, Father.

Scene 13

The bus shelter. The same morning.

Ben [*entering*] Youse look like you've just seen a ghost.
Mark What? Yeah. How are you feeling?
Ben Fine. Mum was just stressing out, that was all. Anything happen while I was sick?
Mark Not much.

Pause.

Ben Why's everyone so early?
Tracey Because Anna's telling us the story.
Ben You still playing The Game?

ANNA nods.

Crikey. It must be a long story.
Tracey Come on, Anna!
Ben Have there been any good bits?
Mark There've just been a couple of bombs.
Ben Doesn't sound like I've missed much.
Fraulein Gelber Sssh.

Scene 14

Germany, April 1945. Leaving the farmhouse.

Planes roar overhead. We hear cars arriving.

The lights change.

Fraulein Gelber Heidi! Come on!
Heidi What is it?
Fraulein Gelber A car has come for us. We have to go. Quickly.
Heidi To see Duffi again?
Fraulein Gelber Perhaps. I don't know. Hurry. *Schnell!*
Heidi To Berlin?
Fraulein Gelber Perhaps. Somewhere safer. The car is waiting. Here is your bag. Quickly.

Heidi Are there soldiers coming, Fraulein Gelber?

Fraulein Gelber Yes. The Russians. They will be here soon.

Heidi What about Frau Leib?

Fraulein Gelber She will have to look after herself. Besides, she will never leave her family.

Heidi What about my rabbits?

Fraulein Gelber Frau Leib will take care of your rabbits.

Heidi My dolls!

Fraulein Gelber Only one. Come now. Hurry. We don't have much time.

They exit in coats and hats with suitcases and Heidi's doll.

Planes roar overhead. Bombs explode. Rumblings of a war zone.

A bomb flashes. Gunfire.

We see FRAULEIN GELBER and HEIDI running through the woods. Their black shadows dance in the moonlight.

These sound and lighting effects crossfade into the sounds of the bunker.

FRAULEIN GELBER and HEIDI enter the bunker, which is the bus shelter lit by a solitary light bulb.

Scene 15

Berlin, April 1945. The bunker.

We hear the sounds of dogs barking, the rumble of bombs above, the sound of a morse code machine working.

A constant, dull, humming noise occurs all through the bunker scene, along with the occasional high-pitched scream of the bombs above. Berlin is falling.

FRAULEIN GELBER and HEIDI arrive dressed in coats and hats and carrying suitcases.

We hear Wagner being played on a gramophone.

Fraulein Gelber There's not much room.

Heidi It's cold.

Fraulein Gelber The walls are damp.

A loud bomb drops. The ceiling lights flicker and the bunker shakes.

FRAULEIN GELBER starts to unpack her suitcase.

You'll be safe down here.

Heidi Is Duffi here?

Fraulein Gelber Yes. Somewhere.

Another loud explosion and the lights flicker once more.

You sleep here.

Heidi When do you think the bombing will stop? Will there be anything left? [*Pause.*] Houses or trees?

A SOLDIER enters, carrying a plate with some bread and a sausage on it. He hands the plate to FRAULEIN GELBER.

When will the bombing stop?

He ignores her and goes to exit.

Soldier!

The SOLDIER stops.

When will the bombing stop?

The SOLDIER exits.

FRAULEIN GELBER divides the sausage and bread and puts some in her pocket.

Fraulein Gelber For later.

HEIDI and FRAULEIN GELBER sit on the bunk and eat the sausage and bread, slowly.

Heidi Does Duffi know we're eating meat?

Fraulein Gelber Shhhh...

Heidi Doesn't taste very nice.

Fraulein Gelber Eat.

They eat in silence.

Dogs barking and the sounds of running and voices (in German) echo in the corridor outside.

FRAULEIN GELBER wraps HEIDI in a blanket on the bed and holds her.

Shhhhhh, we'll try to sleep.

FRAULEIN GELBER tucks up the blanket around HEIDI, makes sure she is asleep, then kisses her, picks up her suitcase and leaves the bunker.

The bus shelter.

BEN interrupts the story.

Ben Is she in Hitler's bunker? Cool. The Russians blew that to smithereens.

Mark Shut up. Let Anna tell the story.

ANNA continues the story. As she speaks, HEIDI plays out the action in the bunker.

Anna Heidi awoke. She didn't know whether it was morning or night. Fraulein Gelber had gone. Heidi was alone.

Heidi Fraulein? Fraulein?

A distant rumble of thunder is heard above the bus shelter and the sound of bombs over the bunker. The sounds of people again in the corridor, hurried footsteps, voices yelling. We hear the frantic voice of HITLER screaming out manically.

Hitler [*voice-over, in German*] *Verräter! Von Anfang an haben mich alle verraten! Sie haben das deutsche Volk verraten! Das werden sie mit ihrem Blut bezahlen, sie werden in ihrem eigenen Blut ertrinken! Wir werden diese Verräter erbarmungslos vernichten! Das ist mein Befehl!* [Traitors! I've been betrayed from the beginning! They have betrayed the German people! These traitors will pay with their blood, they will drown in their own blood! No compassion for the traitors! This is my will!]

HEIDI recognises the voice. She goes out into the corridor following the sound which grows louder as she gets closer to her father.

Another bomb shakes the bunker as HEIDI turns a corner and there is her father, HITLER.

We see the shadow of HITLER.

Heidi Father?

HITLER's voice stops.

Father?

Hitler [*voice-over, in English*] Who is this girl? I've never seen her before. This is no place for a child. Take her away now. Now, do you hear me! Now!

Soldier Yes, *mein Führer.*

He salutes.

The shadow of HITLER disappears. A swastika appears in its place.

A door is heard slamming shut.

The SOLDIER takes HEIDI by the hand and leads her back along the corridors to her bunk bed.

Get your suitcase.

HEIDI does not move. The SOLDIER throws HEIDI's belongings into the suitcase.

Don't be frightened. You're going to good people.

We hear another bomb. The Allies are getting closer.

From the shelter we hear a dog barking frantically and the sound of running footsteps and yelling.

The SOLDIER takes Heidi's suitcase and, holding her hand, they begin their journey to the surface.

As they surface, we simultaneously hear the rumble of the bombs in Berlin and thunder over the bus shelter in Australia. We hear the beginning of rain on the tin roof.

The storm in Australia and the war in Berlin collide.

Throughout the following, the SOLDIER and HEIDI run through the war zone of Berlin, which is falling.

Anna The smell was disgusting as they climbed up to the street.

Soldier They're hitting the sewers.

Anna The world was noise, and rubble and splinters of rocks flew through the air. You could smell the blood and hatred just like you could smell the pigs in Frau Leib's mud.

Soldier This way.

He picks up HEIDI, helping her over the rubble.

Anna There had once been trees and gardens. Now there was just a battle. They ran through the skeleton of the garden, then down, back underground. Along a tunnel now. There were steps but they passed by them, then more steps. They came out at what looked like a railway station.

Soldier They should be here by now. They were supposed to be waiting for you...

We hear the whistle of a bomb dropping. The SOLDIER tries to protect HEIDI with his body.

An explosion.

They get thrown to the ground. The SOLDIER is dead. HEIDI crawls out from under the SOLDIER and touches his face.

We hear the whistle of another impending bomb. HEIDI looks to the sky.

A final explosion.

Blackout.

Silence.

The lights slowly come up, revealing HEIDI standing alone.

Anna Duffi's daughter was gone. The good girl that Fraulein Gelber had tried to make her be was gone.

Mark Are you all right?... Where's your father?

Heidi I have no father. I have no mother. I am alone.

Anna All that was left was Heidi... a small seed deep inside her. All she had to do was survive and that seed could grow.

Scene 16

The bus shelter. Friday morning.

The storm has passed. The children all sit quietly.

Mark What happened then?

Anna Nothing. That's the end of the story.

Tracey But it can't be the end. Please, Anna... where did she go then? Did she find somewhere safe?

Anna After the explosion she was helped by the Schmidt family and went with them to a refugee camp. They made it to the part of Berlin that the Americans controlled.

Mark And then?

Anna And then they came out to Australia.

Tracey Australia?

Mark. You mean here?

Ben But... that's impossible!

Anna No it's not. Lots of refugees came here after World War Two. Herr Schmidt and his family left the refugee camp and they all came out together. He accepted Heidi as his daughter. People had so little then, just their family. Herr Schmidt said Heidi was *'eine gabe von Gott'*. A gift from God.

Mark I didn't know you spoke German.

Anna Just a few words. My grandma taught me. She spoke... a little German.

Ben But she can't have come to Australia. We'd have heard if Hitler's daughter came here.

Mark She's not real. Remember? And anyway, no one knew she was Hitler's daughter, did they, Anna?

ANNA shakes her head.

Anna She went to school in Australia. It took her longer to get through school than others, because she'd missed so much, and she had to learn English, too. Then she went to university. She became a doctor, a pediatrician.

Tracey Did she get married?

Anna She married another doctor and she had children.

Ben Hitler's grandchildren!

Anna No, Heidi's children.

Ben What did her kids do?

Anna One became a furniture maker and the other one... I don't know.

Mark But it's your story. You have to know!

Tracey A teacher. The other one became a teacher.

Anna Okay, a teacher.

Ben Imagine being Hitler's grandkid.

The bus is heard arriving, along with the soft beginning of rain.

Bus! Race ya, Trace.

BEN and TRACEY exit.

Mark Anna?

Anna Mmm?

Mark Did... did Heidi ever tell anyone? About who her father was?

Anna How could she tell anyone? She'd have been hated, just like her father was hated.

Mark But it wasn't her fault.

Anna Who'd have believed that? Besides, she wanted a new life... a real life, like everyone else, with a family and friends to laugh with.

Mark You mean she kept quiet? She never told anybody at all? [*Pause.*] Anna?

Anna What?

Mark I see why she couldn't tell anyone. No one would understand, not really. She'd be afraid they'd see Hitler, not her.

Anna She'd just be Hitler's daughter. All her life...

Mark I just thought... that maybe... maybe sometimes she couldn't keep it to herself. That she'd have to tell someone... just once.

Anna She told her granddaughter. Just once, like you said. One day when it was raining, like today. It was just before she died. She told her all about Fraulein Gelber and Frau Mundt and Frau Leib. But it was just a story. That's what she told her granddaughter. Only a story. Just pretend. That's all.

Mark Just pretend.

ANNA nods and she exits.

From off stage we hear HEIDI singing the last two lines of 'Twinkle Twinkle Little Star' in German.

Heidi *Funkel, funkel, kleiner Stern,*
Ach wie bist du mir so fern.

MARK looks out.

The cows are mooing.

The lights fade to black.

THE END